Beautiful CORK and KERRY

Featuring the photography of Michael Diggin,
Bord Fáilte and Colour Library Books Ltd

Published in Ireland by Gill and Macmillan Ltd
Goldenbridge
Dublin 8

With associated companies in Auckland, Budapest, Gaborone, Harare, Hong Kong, Kampala, Kuala Lumpur, Lagos, London, Madras, Manzini, Melbourne, Mexico City, Nairobi, New York, Singapore, Sydney, Tokyo, Windhoek

Printed and bound in Singapore by Tien Wah Press
ISBN 0 7171 2067 8

Beautiful
CORK and KERRY

Gill and Macmillan

Reaching out into the Atlantic, the southern counties of Cork and Kerry resist the staunch battering of the Atlantic Ocean and shelter the charm and culture of the people. In many ways the region might be said to epitomise Ireland, for crowded into this small corner of the land are many of the features which make Ireland Irish.

The three peninsulas of Dingle, Iveragh and Beara boast arguably the finest scenery to be found anywhere in Ireland. Certainly the tourist coaches which ply endlessly around Iveragh in the summer months indicate that it is the most popular. The towering mountains of the interior plunge dramatically into the ocean to form great cliffs and sheer hillsides, and the soft light peculiar to late afternoon here makes for truly entrancing landscapes.

Dingle Peninsula is, itself, almost the epitome of rural Ireland. It is here that quaint cottages are most likely to be found amid scattered ruins of the early Celtic Christianity which was once the cultural splendour of the region. The Gaelic language is still often heard in Dingle, an indication of the resilience of local culture to change. Beara, the southernmost of the three peninsulas, is easily the wildest and most remote. Even the buses run on only four days a week.

Inland the landscapes of Kerry are less wild, but no less enchanting, and a popular and impressive route from the Iveragh to Killarney is through the Gap of Dunloe. This dramatic gash in the mountains known as Macgillycuddy's Reeks is traversed only by an unmade road, which is usually crowded with pony traps taking visitors to see the spectacle.

The town of Killarney, east of the Gap of Dunloe, is surrounded by some of the finest lakeland scenery in Europe, and Lough Leane is the greatest of the lakes here. Its spreading waters are backed by some of the highest peaks in the country, though at little over 3,000 feet they are still not out of proportion to the gentle landscape.

South into Cork both the scenery and atmosphere change distinctively. Most of the land is less dramatic than that of Kerry, but no less Irish. At the heart of Cork lies Blarney Castle, possibly the best-known ruin in Ireland. The fame of the fortress dates back to the late 16th century, when MacCarthy, Lord of Blarney, professed loyalty to Queen Elizabeth of England. However, when Elizabeth sent messengers to MacCarthy he always promised action and money without ever actually supplying either. When yet another emissary returned with fine promises, the Queen is said to have dismissed the man with scant ceremony. 'It is the usual Blarney,' she said. Today, the keepers of the castle show visitors the legendary Blarney Stone, which is said to confer on any who kiss it the almost magical, persuasive abilities of the original MacCarthy of Blarney. There is certainly some magic, for thousands are persuaded to part with their money each year to kiss the stone. The nearby wool mill profits quite nicely from tourists, too.

In many ways Blarney is typical of the Cork countryside. It is full of history and is immersed in the semi-legendary story of Celtic Ireland, yet it is fully awake to the modern world. Youghal has long been a prosperous seaside town. The medieval city walls and magnificent, 18th-century houses proclaim its former glory as a port city. Though today the port is too small to handle international trade, the town continues to thrive as a holiday resort due to its fine beaches and strong music tradition.

Cork City itself is proud of its reputation as the cultural capital of Ireland. Though this is a title which Cork gave itself, the outsider will certainly find the city vibrant and lively. The old town boasts not only the types of shops common elsewhere, but also smart French fashion houses, a large flea market and transatlantic fast food stores. Indeed, the people of Cork have long had strong links outside Ireland, for this town was once the largest export port for dairy produce in Europe, and the old Butter Market is now beautifully restored.

West Cork is something else again. The warm and wet climate combine with poor soil to provide a traditionally rich but precarious society. When the potato famines struck, West Cork was hit worse than most other areas. Though people have traditionally emigrated from the region, in recent years the flow has been the other way. Many Dutch, Germans and British have come to settle. Known locally as 'blow-ins', the strangers have become part of the local community.

The landscape of West Cork is truly breathtaking. Not as toweringly dramatic as the west coast of Kerry, it is none the less equally impressive. The wild seas of Bantry and Roaring Water Bay hurl themselves on the rugged shoreline behind which shelter charming villages and ancient ruins. As with so much of Cork and Kerry the area has a unique charm which many who visit find irresistible.

No wonder the 'blow-ins' rarely go home.

Left: The lighthouse at Youghal, County Cork. The town is now a charming seaside resort, and its fine, historical buildings are testimony to its former wealth and power as a major port city.
Overleaf: Scenery around Youghal.

Above: Blarney Castle, home in the 16th century to Dermot MacCarthy, the wily chief of Muskerry who kept both sides happy in the wars with soft words. **Right:** Kissing the Blarney Stone, said to confer the power of persuasive speech.

THERE IS NO CHARGE FOR
KISSING THE BLARNEY STONE
REMOVE ALL LOOSE VALUABLES
BEFORE DOING SO

These pages: Blarney Castle House, which stands near the largely ruined Blarney Castle. Built in the 19th century as a comfortable mansion with a traditional exterior, the house is now open to the public.

BELL

SLV

No.1
CHAPEL STREET
THE STAR.
SILK CUT

Top left: A brightly coloured display in Kinsale, an attractive little town rich in history, on the banks of the River Bandon. **Left and above:** The streets of Cork. **Overleaf:** A small shop near Cobh, the leading port of the south of Ireland.

Sandqua
BURGOLARM

sno
WHIP
Real!
Dairy
Ice Cream
CMP DAIRY
Approved Quality System

Stores
HOMESTEAD
BRINGS VALUE HOME
REHAB
LOTTERIES
Great prizes and a good cause
BREAD & CAKES
SWEETS
GROCERY
NEWSPAPERS
FRUIT & VEG
TAYTO
SNAPS
Pickled Onion flavour corn snacks
Tayto
CHIPSTICKS
BAG O'CHIPS
PIZZA TURTLES
CRISPY BACON SNACKS
HOMESTEAD
BRINGS VALUE HOME

Cork City. **Left:** A view down Patrick's Hill towards MacCurtain Street. **Below:** The busy South Mall beside Parliament Bridge. **Facing page:** Saint Finbarr's Cathedral, designed by William Burgess and richly decorated by local and Italian craftsmen. **Overleaf:** The broad thoroughfare of Grand Parade.

STONE T.V.
The Atlantic Inn

These pages: The town of Cobh, with its fine, deep-water harbour. Cobh was a frequent calling place for luxury liners, and in 1915 survivors from the torpedoed liner *Lusitania* were brought here by fishing smacks.

Right: Kinsale Harbour on the estuary of the Bandon River. The sheltered waters are today used most often by pleasure craft and yachts, but until the early 19th century ocean-going craft were handled and much trade passed through here. **Overleaf:** Charles Fort, Kinsale, occupied by James II during his disastrous attempt to regain the throne, which ended on the banks of the Boyne.

Left: Bleak moorland above the fishing town of Baltimore.
Below and facing page: The Grotto of the Virgin at Ballinspittle, near Kinsale. In recent years the grotto has become famous for apparently miraculous movements of the statue on quiet nights. **Overleaf:** The prehistoric stone circle of Drombeg, near Glandore, the purpose of which is as enigmatic as that of the many other circles in the area.

Facing page: Mizen Head, where the cliffs can rise to 700 feet. This is generally taken to be the southwestern extremity of Ireland.
Left, below and overleaf: Scenes near Mizen Head and Crookhaven.

Top left: The Glengarriff Valley. In places, the mild climate of this sheltered but rugged valley allows keen gardeners to grow palms. **Left:** The bare heights of Knocknagallaum. **Above:** The heather-covered Sheehy Mountains. **Overleaf:** A view across the Beara Peninsula.

Top left: Glenmore Lake in the Healy Pass, which runs beneath Ballaghscart to link Adrigole and Lauragh. **Left:** A bridge carries the road up to Healy Pass. **Above:** Mountains near Lauragh. **Overleaf:** The Calvary scene at the top of Healy Pass.

Right: Kenmare, a small town which dates almost exclusively from Victorian times, is a noted tourist centre, for it offers easy access to the Ring of Kerry, Macgillycuddy's Reeks and the Kerry Hills. Outside money has led to a profusion of shops and bars which either make or mar the town, depending on your viewpoint.
Overleaf: The mouth of the Kenmare River.

FOLEY'S
GUEST HOUSE
RESTAURANT
PUB
Dutch
Restaurant
The Purple Heather
IRISH
BAR
HB
100 FZK

These pages: Views of Sneem, a recent winner of Kerry's best-kept village award. The village has the advantage of having been laid out to a regular plan by a benevolent 18th-century owner to provide better quality housing for his tenants.
Overleaf: The romantic landscape near Parknasilla.

THE GREEN HOUSE
BED & BREAKFAST
Tea Rooms

ERIN
Country
KNITWEAR
OFFICE
SHOP ENTRANCE
QUILLS
for
Selection
Quality &
Best Prices
in Ireland
aran handknits
SHOP ENTRANCE
QUILLS WOOLLEN MARKET

Left: The wooded slopes of the hills known as Macgillycuddy's Reeks. **Above:** A cottage nestles into the hillside for shelter from the wind on Knocknagallaum. **Overleaf:** A roadside lough on the Ring of Kerry.

Top left: Derrynane, a popular region for holidaymakers. **Left:** Cattle graze on Scarriff Island, an area known for the quality and range of its seafood. **Above:** Holiday caravans cluster around the fine beach at Westcove, Glenbeigh.

Above: Derrynane Harbour, near which lived the patriot Daniel O'Connell. **Top right and right:** Gorse-spotted fields near Ballybrack, a region famous for fine angling and grouse shooting. **Overleaf:** A view from the 700-feet-high Coomakista Pass on the Ring of Kerry.

Left: The spectacular Ladies View of Killarney. The magnificent scenery around Killarney has turned it from an ordinary mid-Victorian country town into a major tourist centre. **Overleaf:** Carrantuohill, at 3,414 feet the tallest peak in Ireland, in the Macgillycuddy's Reeks.

Facing page: Torc Waterfall near Killarney, down which plunge the waters of the Devil's Punchbowl. **Right:** Kate Kearney's Cottage in Killarney. **Below:** The Gap of Dunloe, a scenic high pass which is accessible only by pony trap or on foot, as the road is impassable to motor vehicles.

Left: Muckross House, Killarney, a fine, 19th-century mansion which has been converted into a folk museum. The gardens are especially charming and well cared for. **Overleaf:** Muckross Abbey, a Franciscan foundation of the 15th century, which was burnt by Cromwellian troopers.

Top left: Rolling grazing land bordering Dingle Bay. **Left:** A view across Smerwick Harbour towards the Three Sisters, scene of a Spanish invasion in 1579. **Above:** A scene near Slea Head, off which lie the Blasket Islands.

Above: Clogher Head on the Dingle Peninsula. **Top right:** A traditional curragh being carried ashore. **Right:** The rocky coast of Dingle. **Overleaf:** Doom Point.
Final page: Soft landscapes of Kerry.

Carnuntum: Pagans' Gate.

PETRONELL (NE)

In the excavations at the Roman town of **Carnuntum,** the ancient capital of Panonia, outstanding are the *Pagans' Gate,* the *Amphitheatre* and the ruins of the old town and the fort. The admirably high quality construction work which went into the baths, heating, water network and canals can be appreciated here.

Carnuntum: the Amphitheatre.

Carnuntum: Spa Hotel.

Our Pay-One-Price Entrance-Fee Includes:

6 km Drive-Through-Safari-Park with animals roaming free, admission tobenteuer-Park with Pet's Corner, Adventure Play-ground and all Shows:

- Acapulco High Diving
- Wet Sealion Show
- Lions and Tigers
- Peppy Parrot's Revue
- Snakes on Parade
- Puma Training
- Bear's Gym
- Funny Pigmy Goats

Sunset over the woods and city of Vienna.

MAYERLING CASTLE

Separated from the Cistercian monastery of Heiligenkreuz by a beautiful forested valley, in the midst of the densest, most romantic woodlands imaginable, stands the historic castle of Mayerling. In 1889 the Archduke Rudolf (the Emperor Franz Josef I's only son and, therefore, heir to the throne of the Austro-Hungarian Empire) and his lover, the young Baroness Maria Vetsera, committed suicide in the hunting lodge here. These romantic, mysterious deaths shook late 19th-century Europe. The double suicide had far-reaching political consequences since with it the sovereign of one of the empires most vital to the stability of Europe at that time, Franz Josef I, was left without a direct successor to his throne.

After the sensational double suicide Mayerling Castle was converted, by decision of the Emperor Franz Josef, into a Carmelite convent.

It is now one of the most popular tourist sites in the environs of Vienna. The surroundings are really extremely beautiful, and in perfect harmony with the tragic atmosphere left by the suicide of the archduke and his lover. Historians, novelists and film-makers have on many occasions given their attention to Mayerling, attempting — with greater or lesser degrees of success and realism — to unravel the mystery that the Archduke Rudolf took with him to his grave.

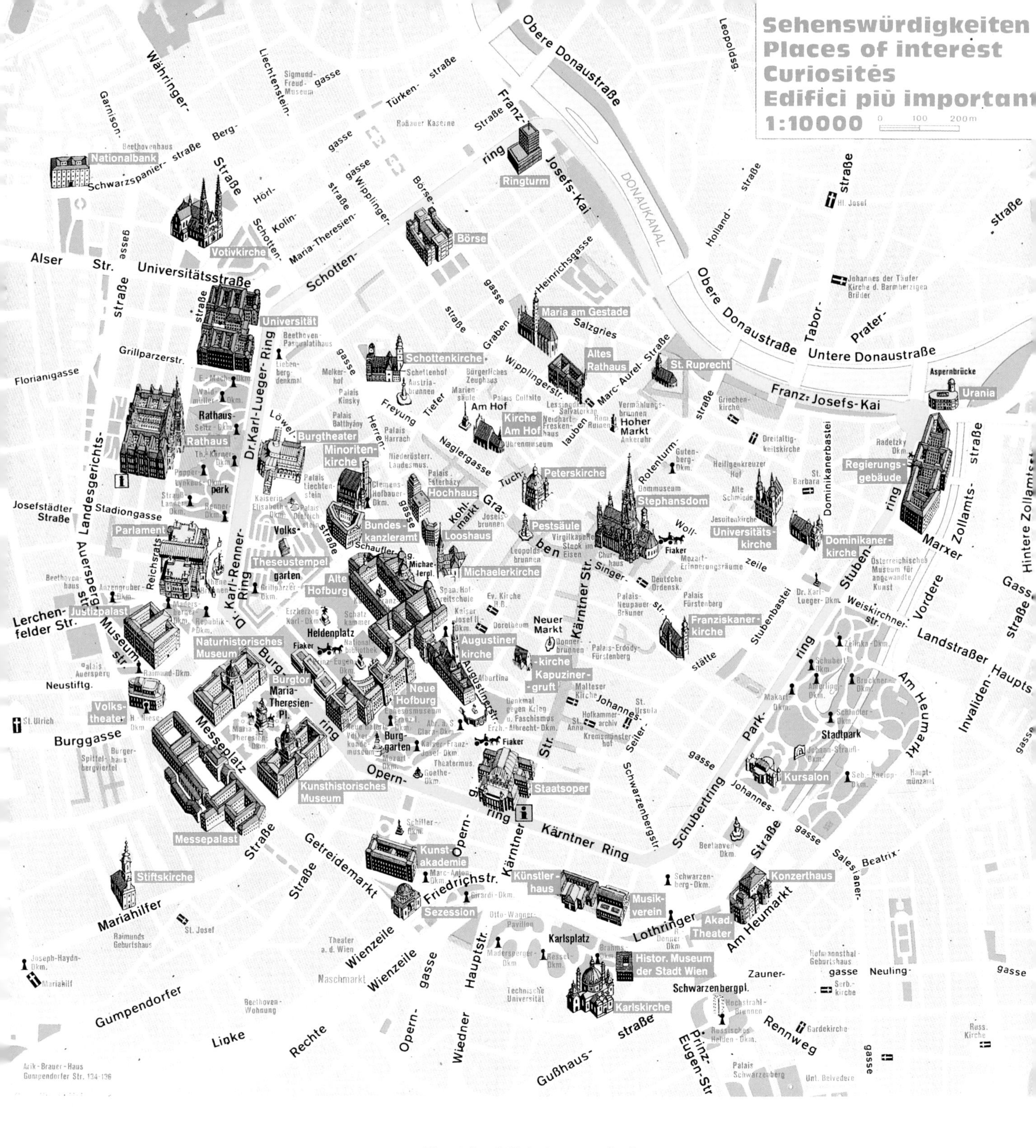

The printing of this book was completed
in the workshops of
FISA - ESCUDO DE ORO, S.A.
Palaudarias, 26 - Barcelona (Spain)